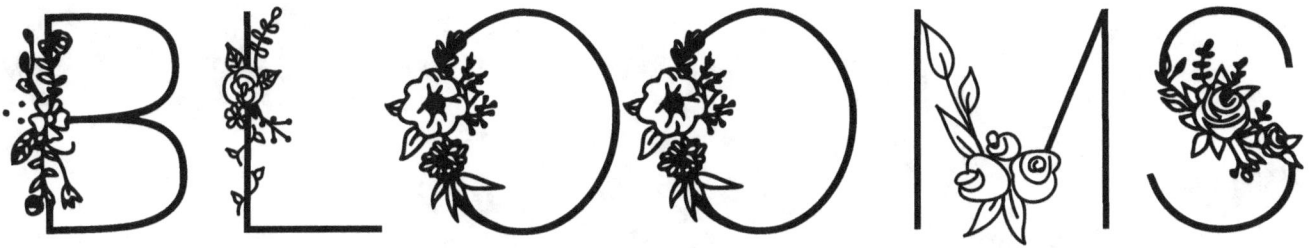

BLOOMS

A floral mandala coloring book

Hand drawn by Tammy Wolski

www.instagram.com/thldesign

fb.me/BloomsColoringBook

Front and back cover designed by www.canva.com

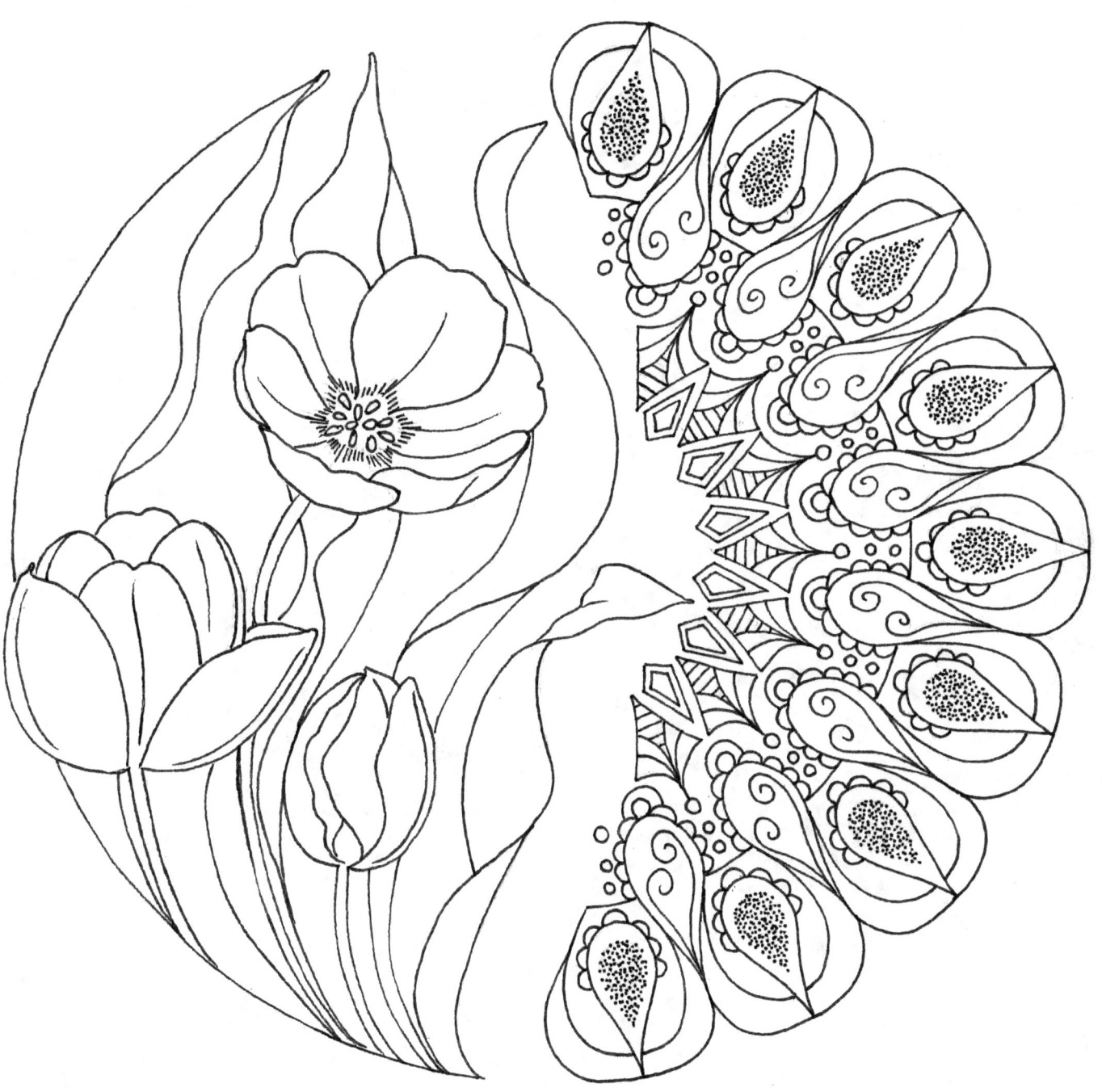

Tulips (Tulipa)

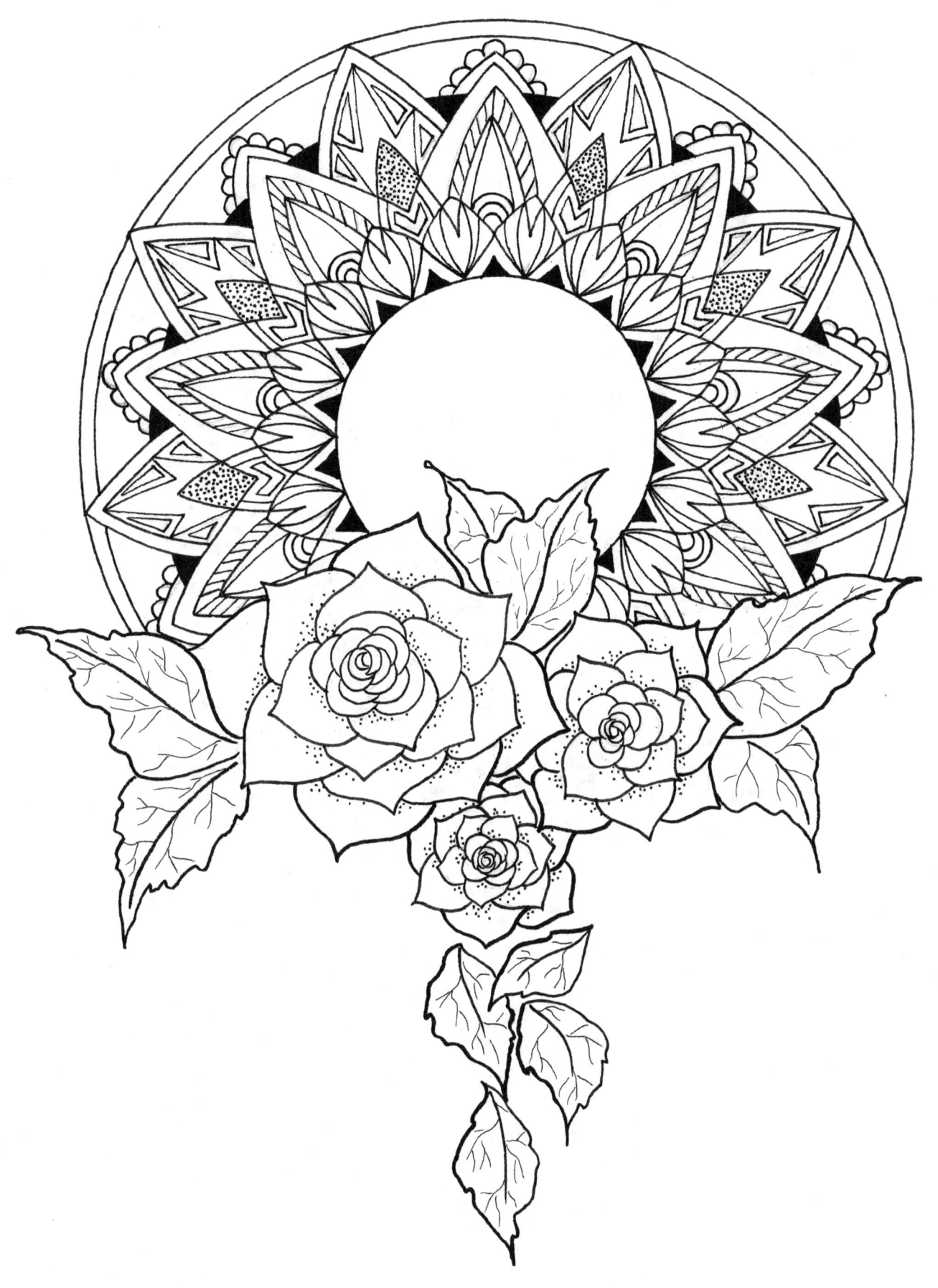

Rose (Rosaceae)

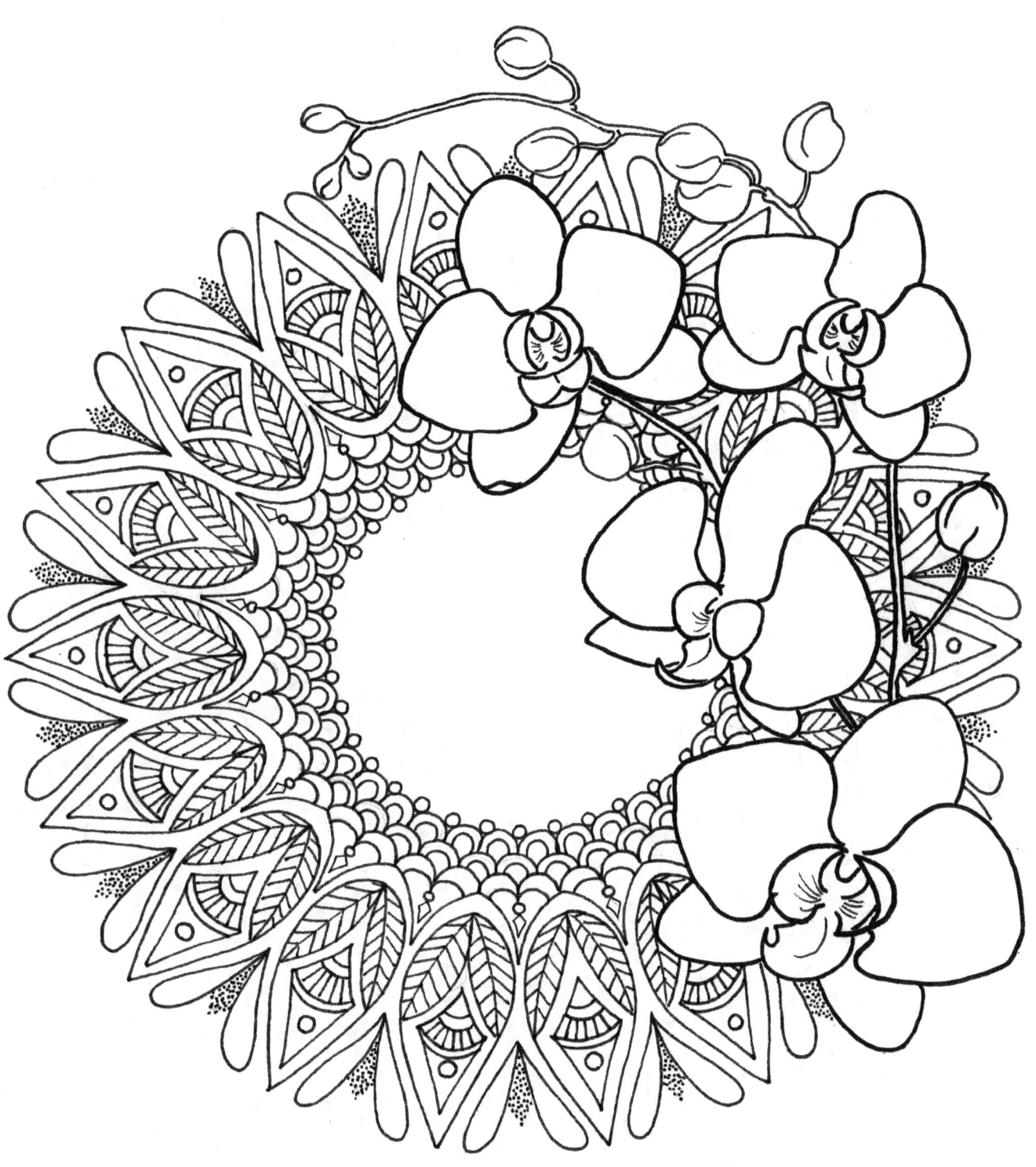

Orchid (Orchidaceae)

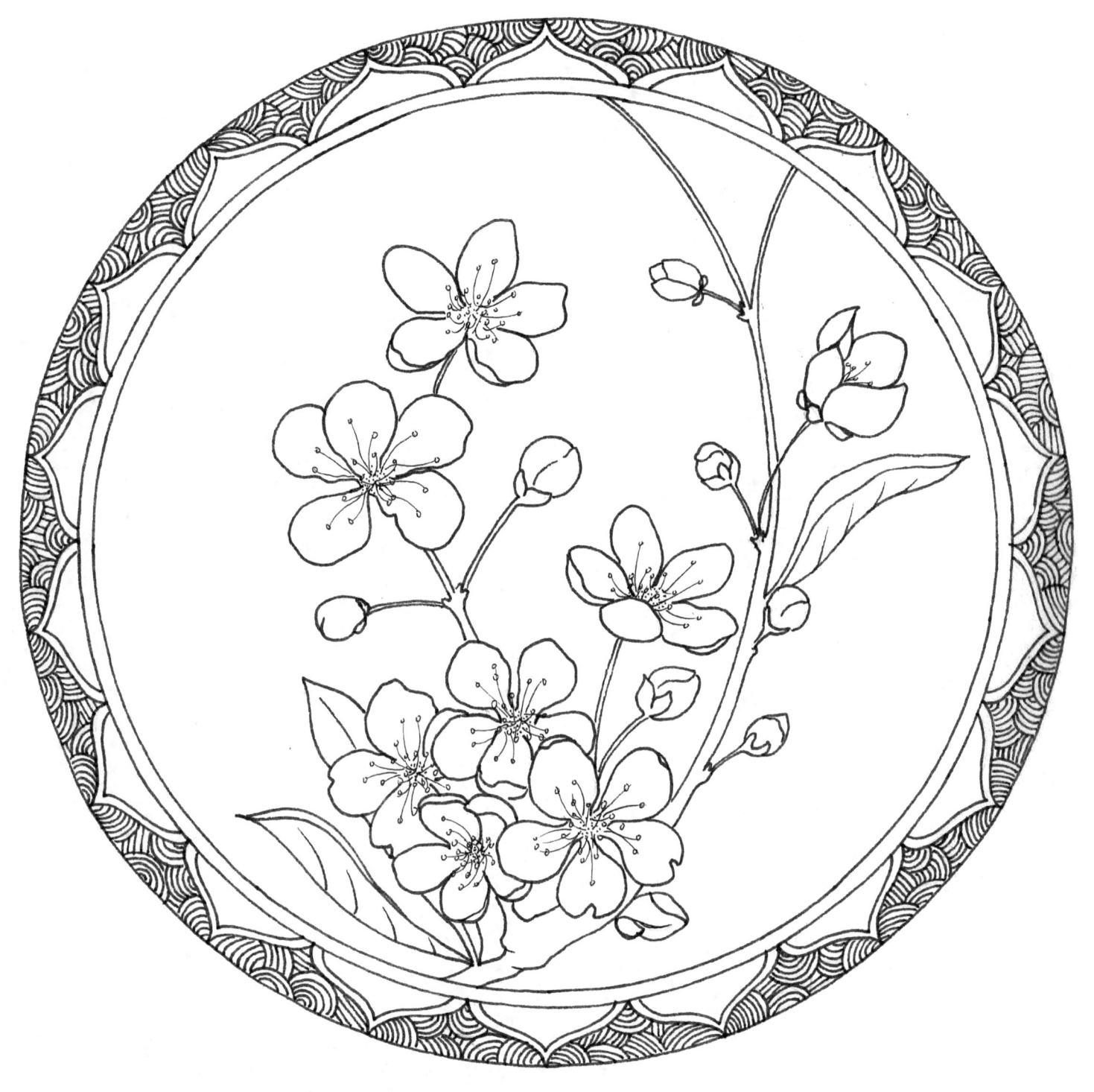

Sakura (Prunus Serrulata)

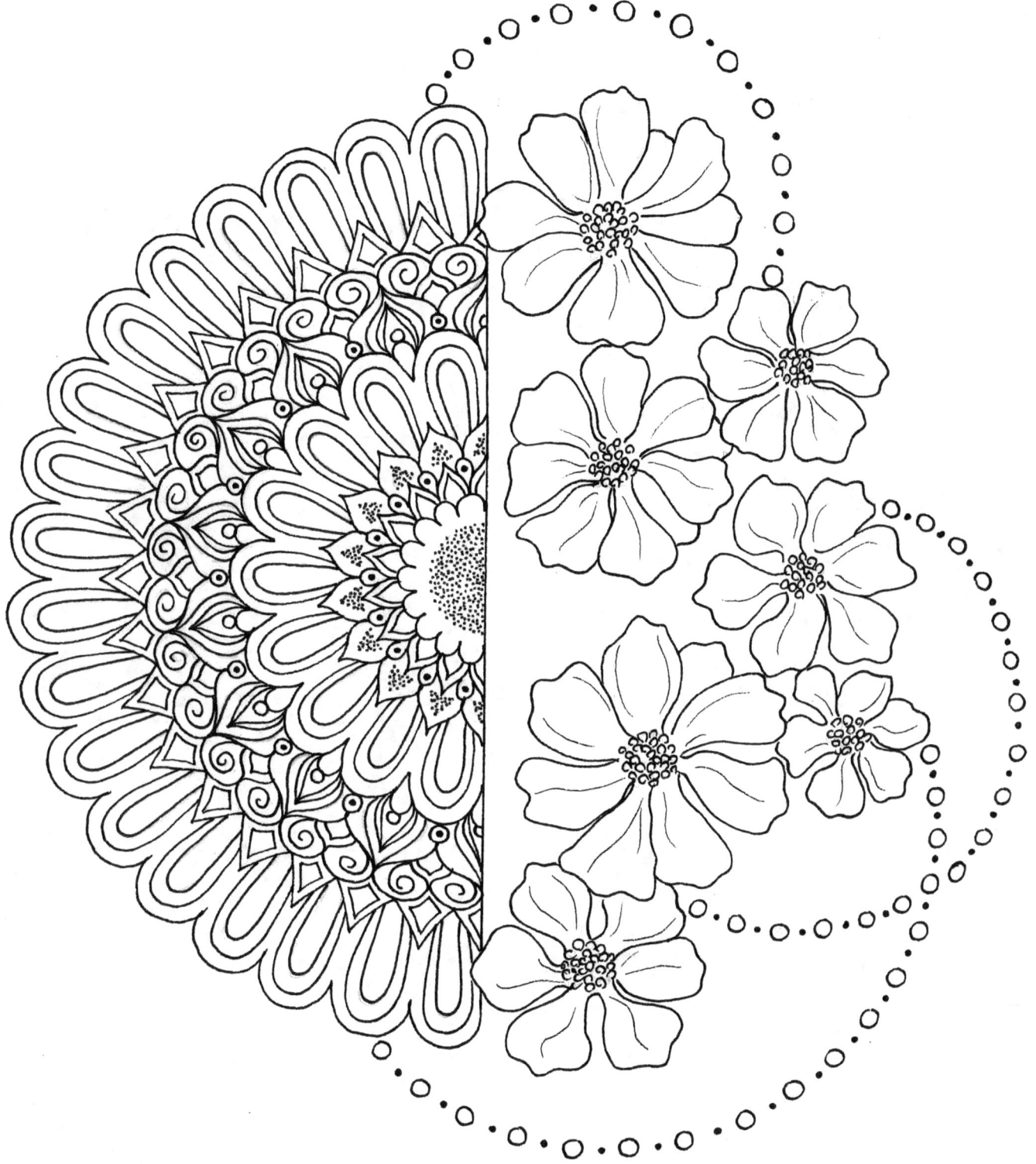

Cosmos (Coreopsideae)

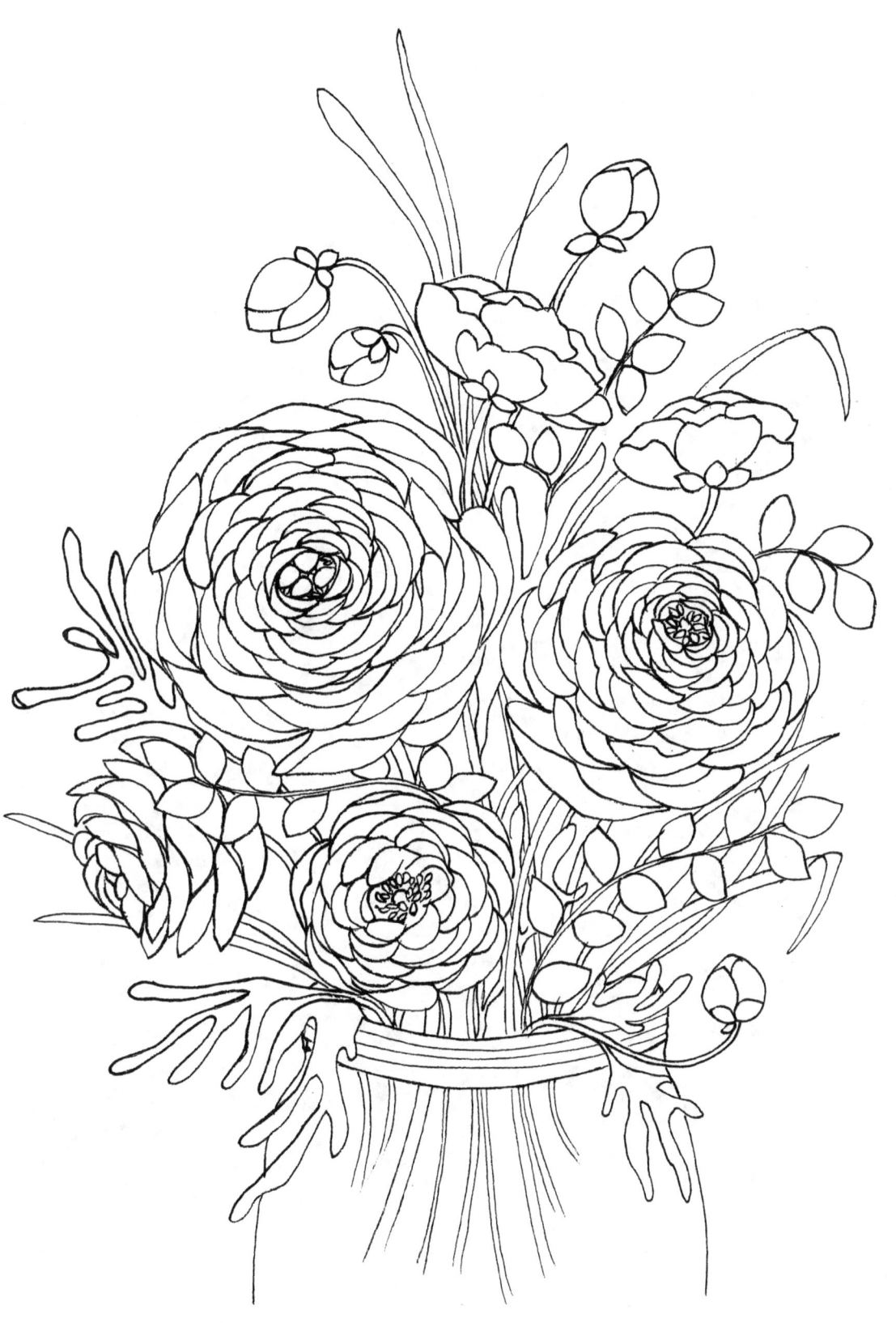

Ranunculus (Ranunculaceae)

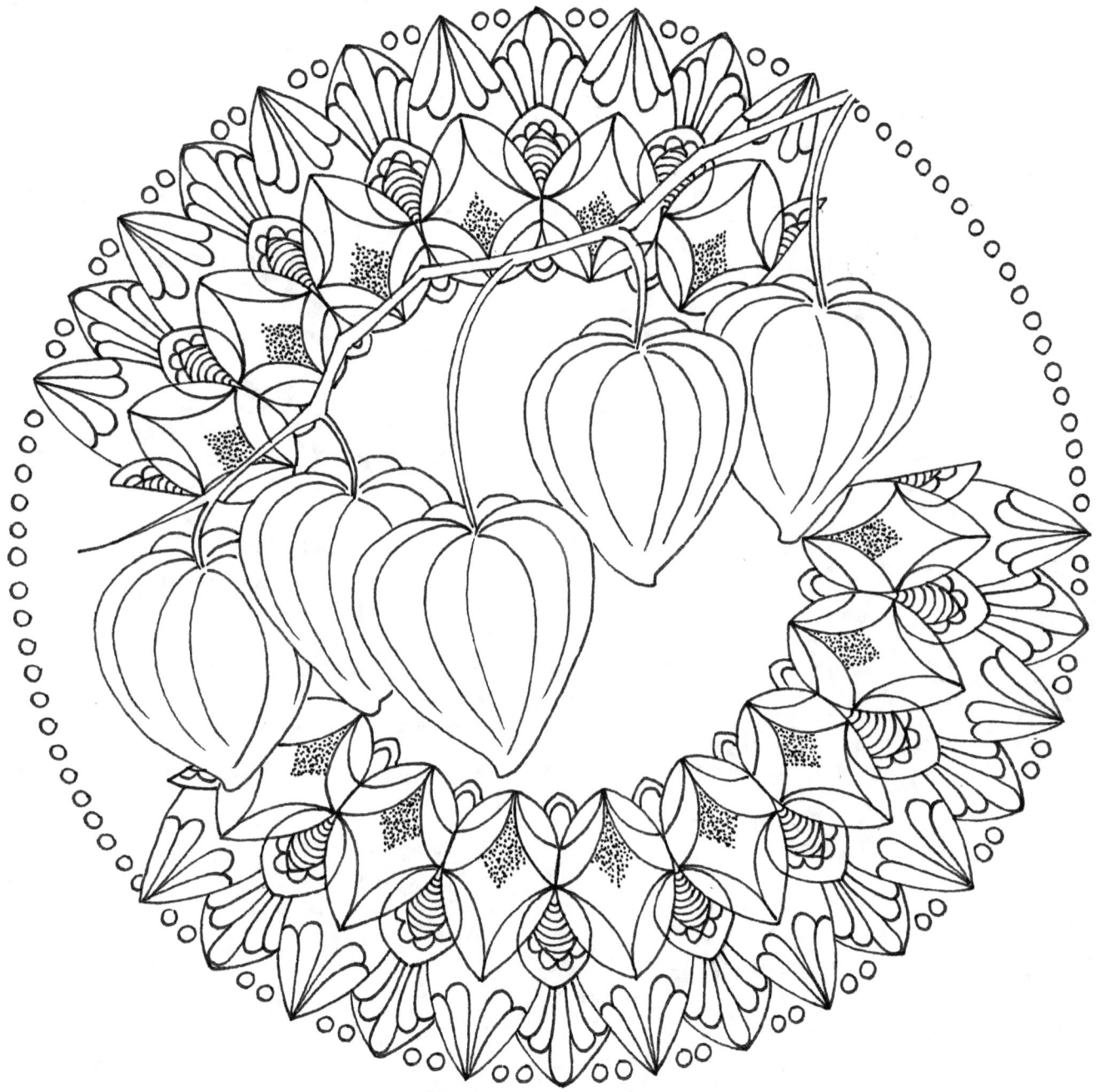

Chinese Lantern (Physalis Alkekengi)

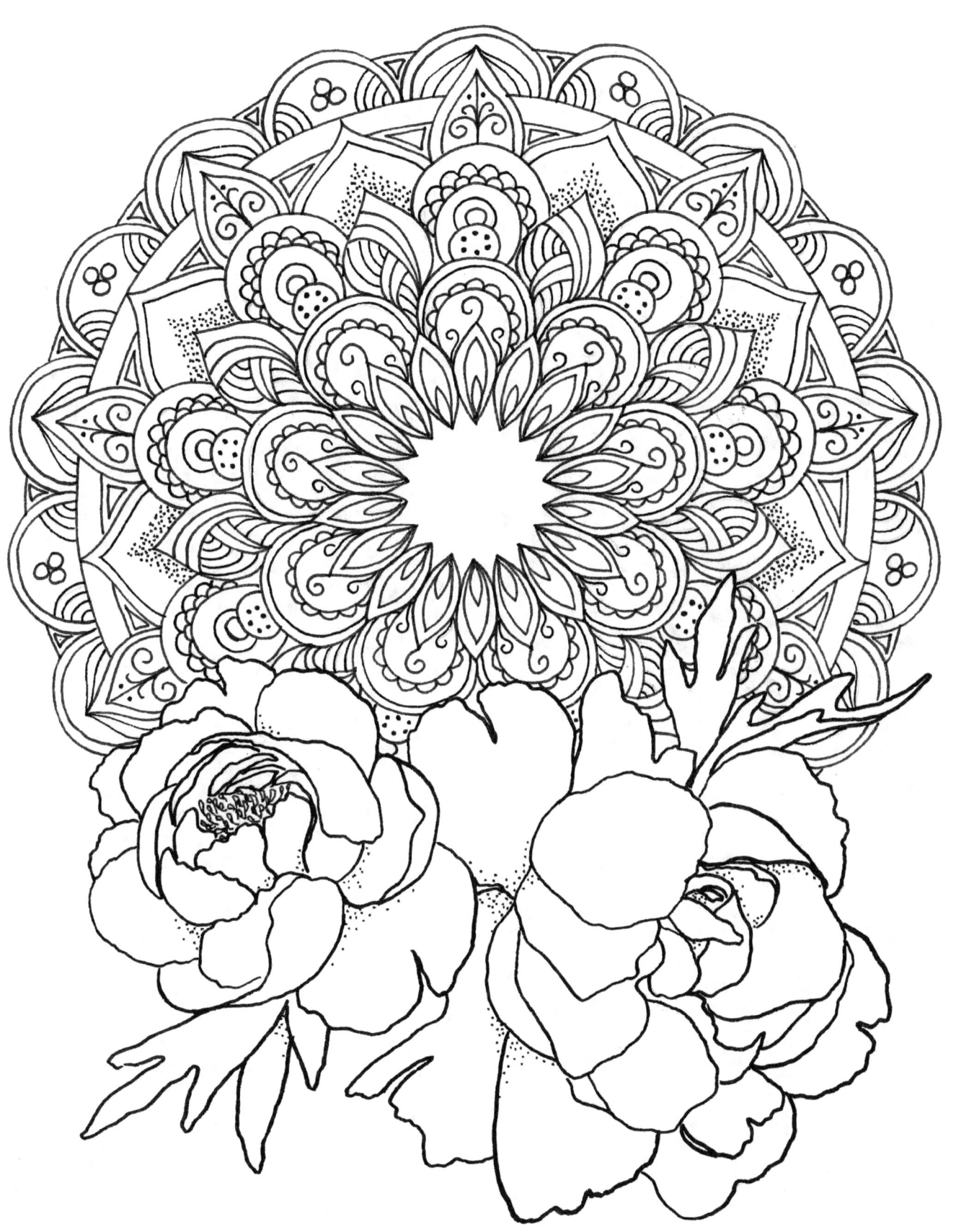

Peony (Paeoniaceae)

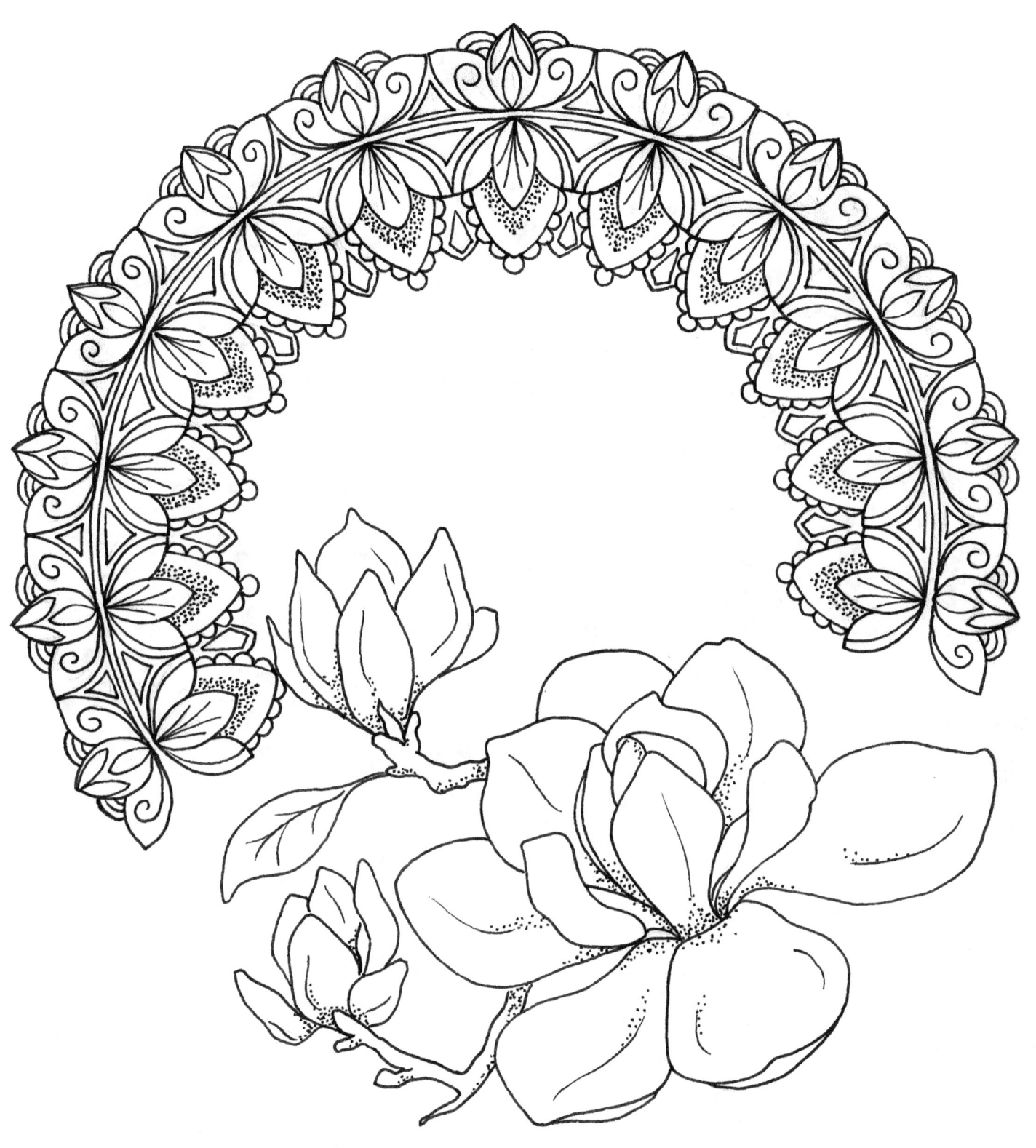

Magnolia (Magnolioideae)

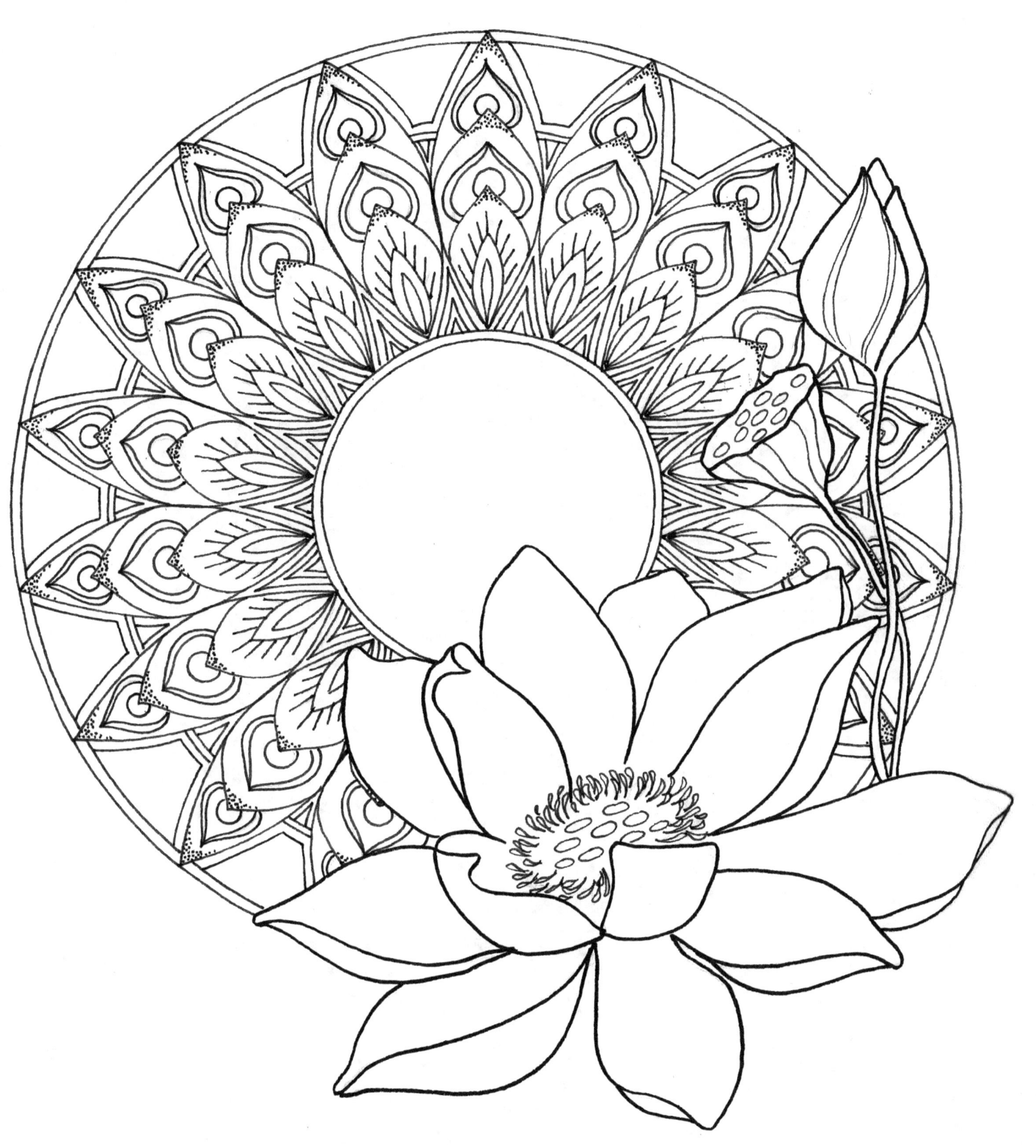

Lotus (Nelumbo Nucifera)

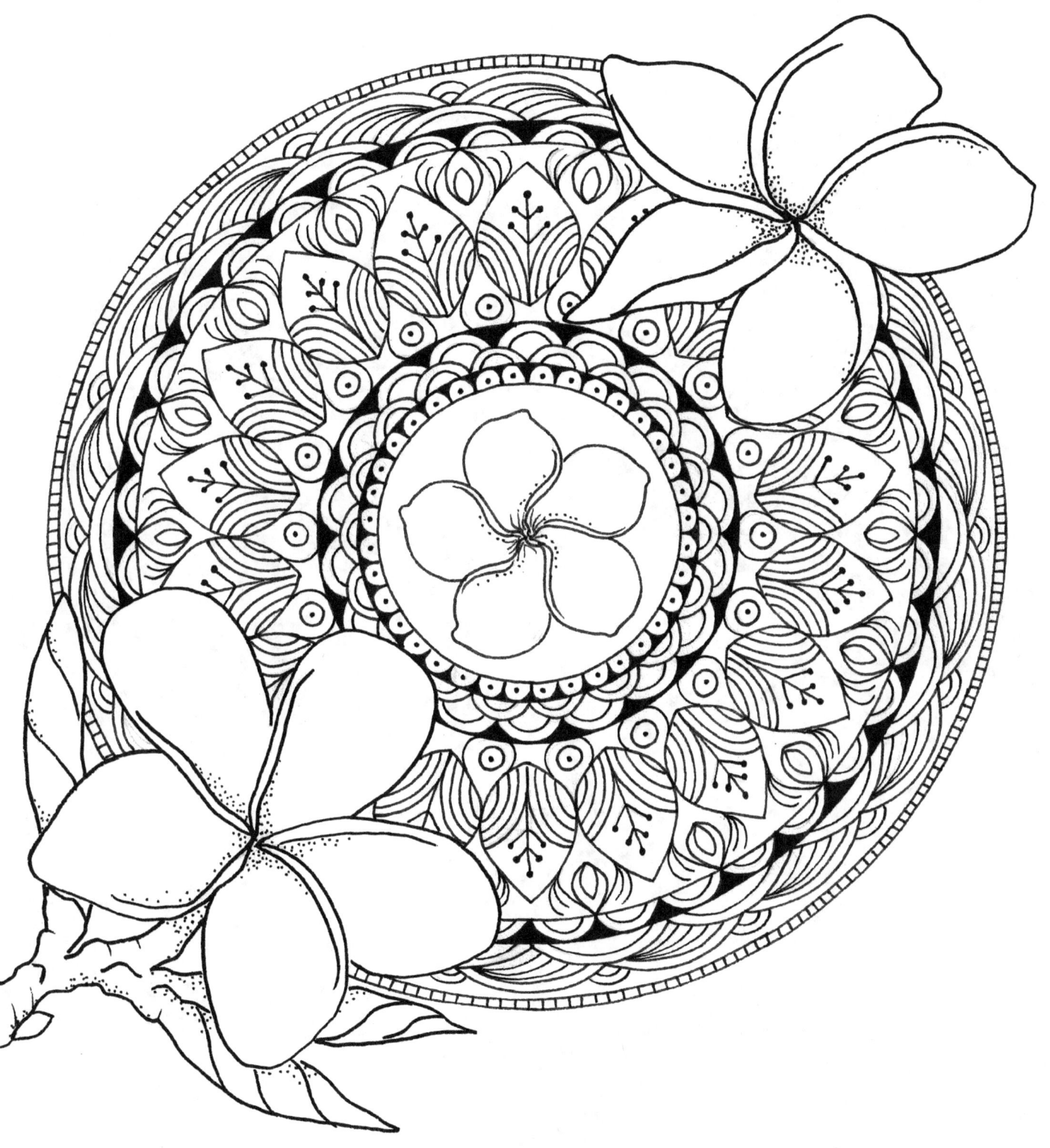

Plumeria (Frangipani)

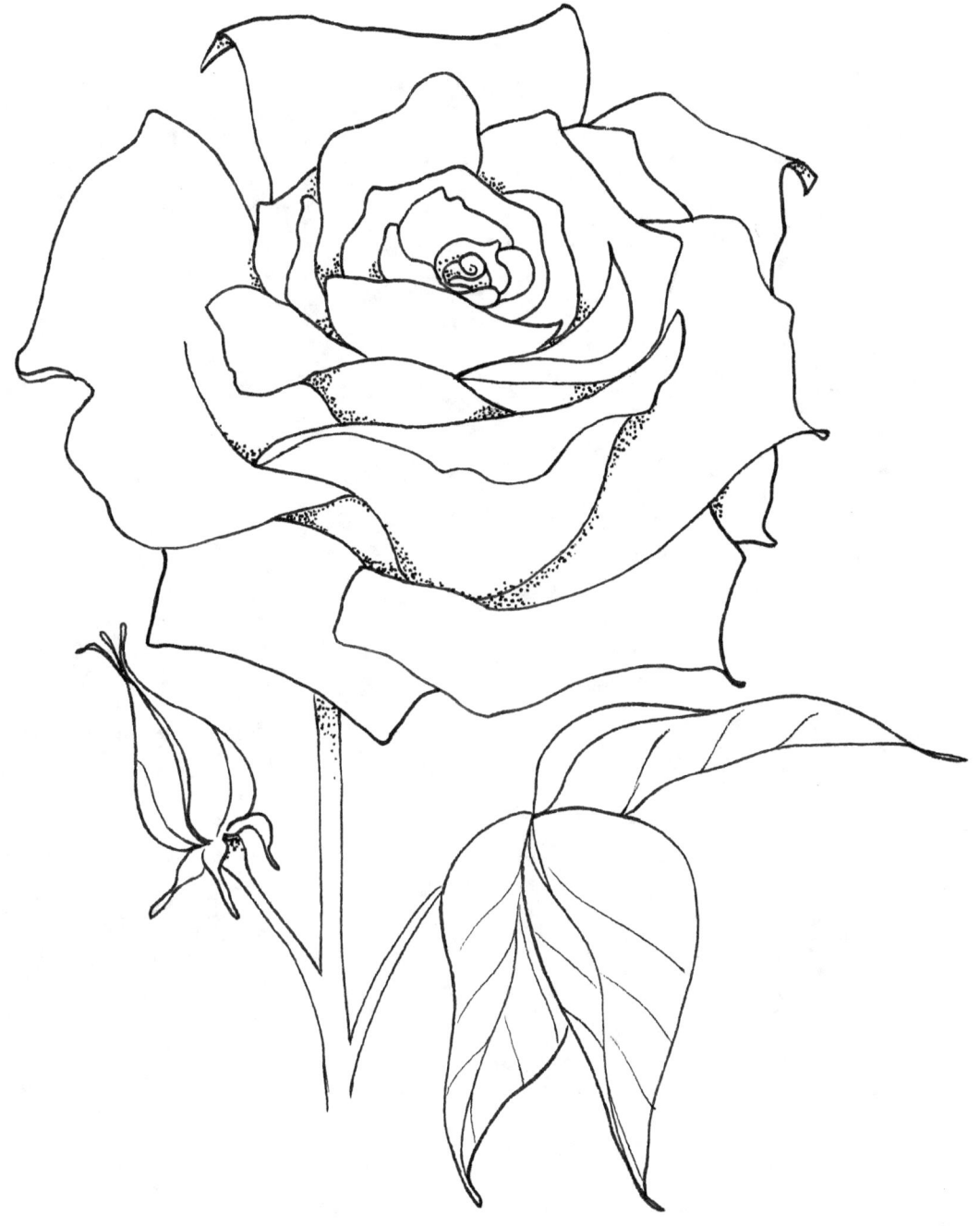

Rose (Rosaceae)

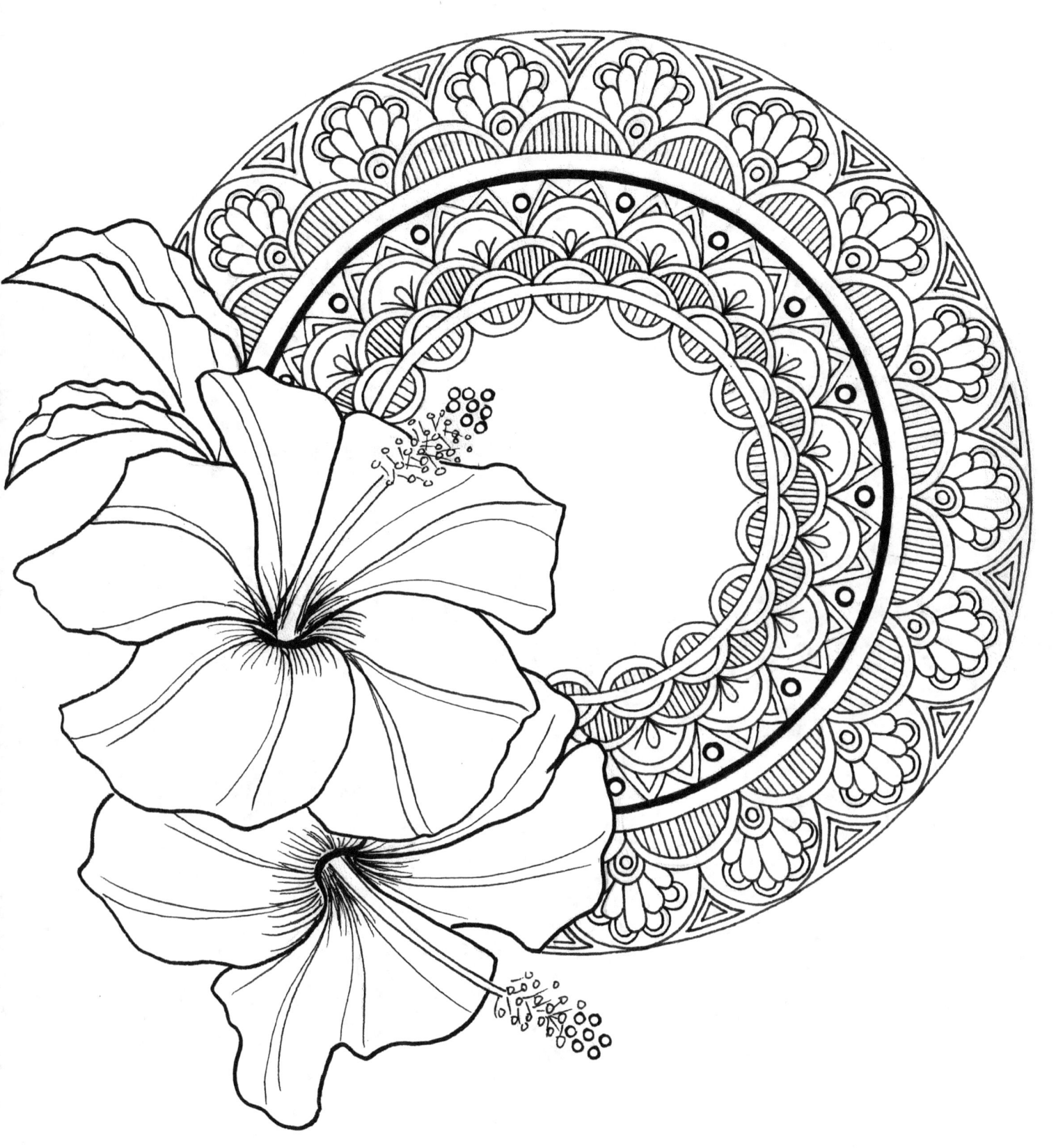

Hibiscus (Malvaceae)

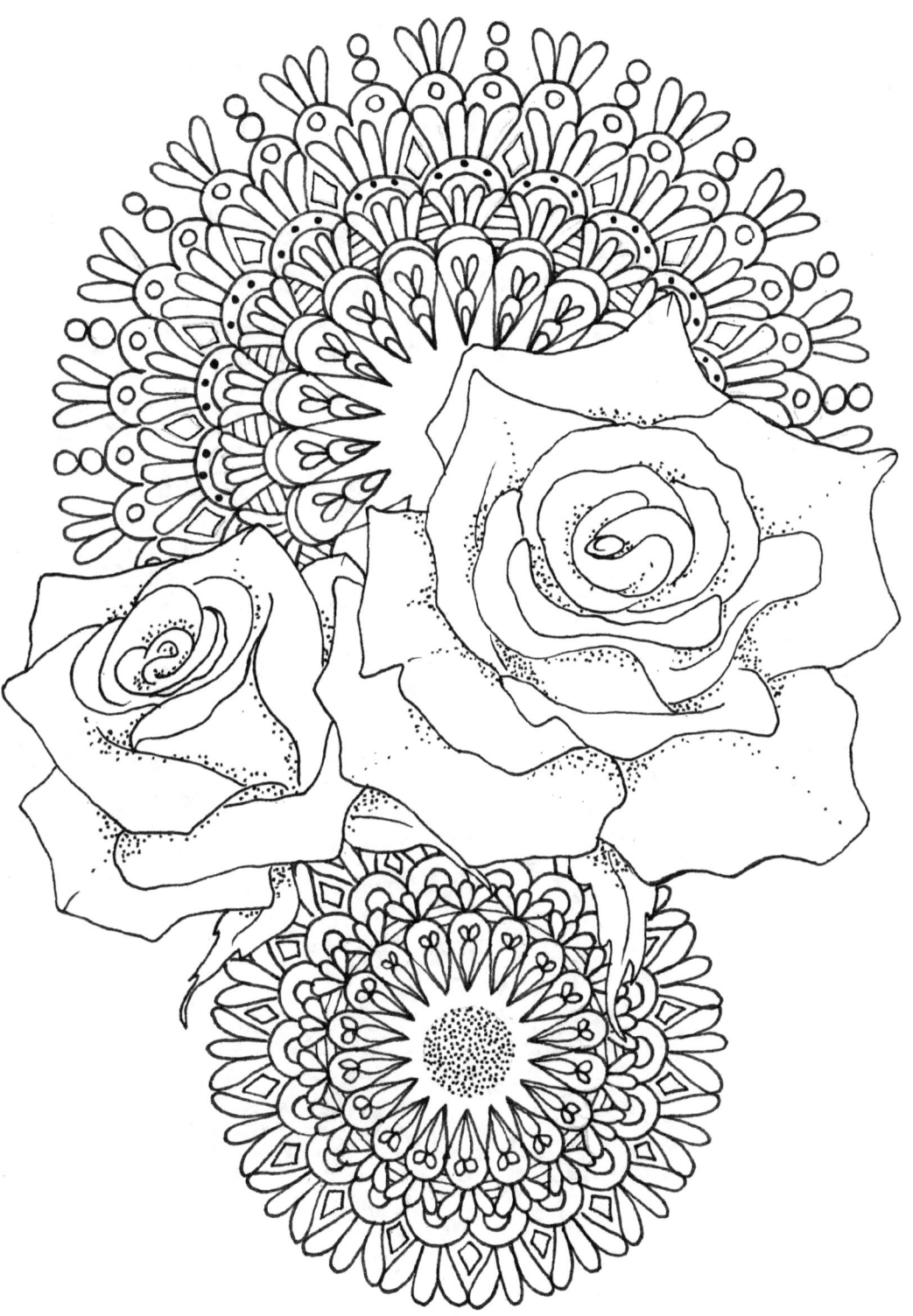

Rose (Rosaceae)

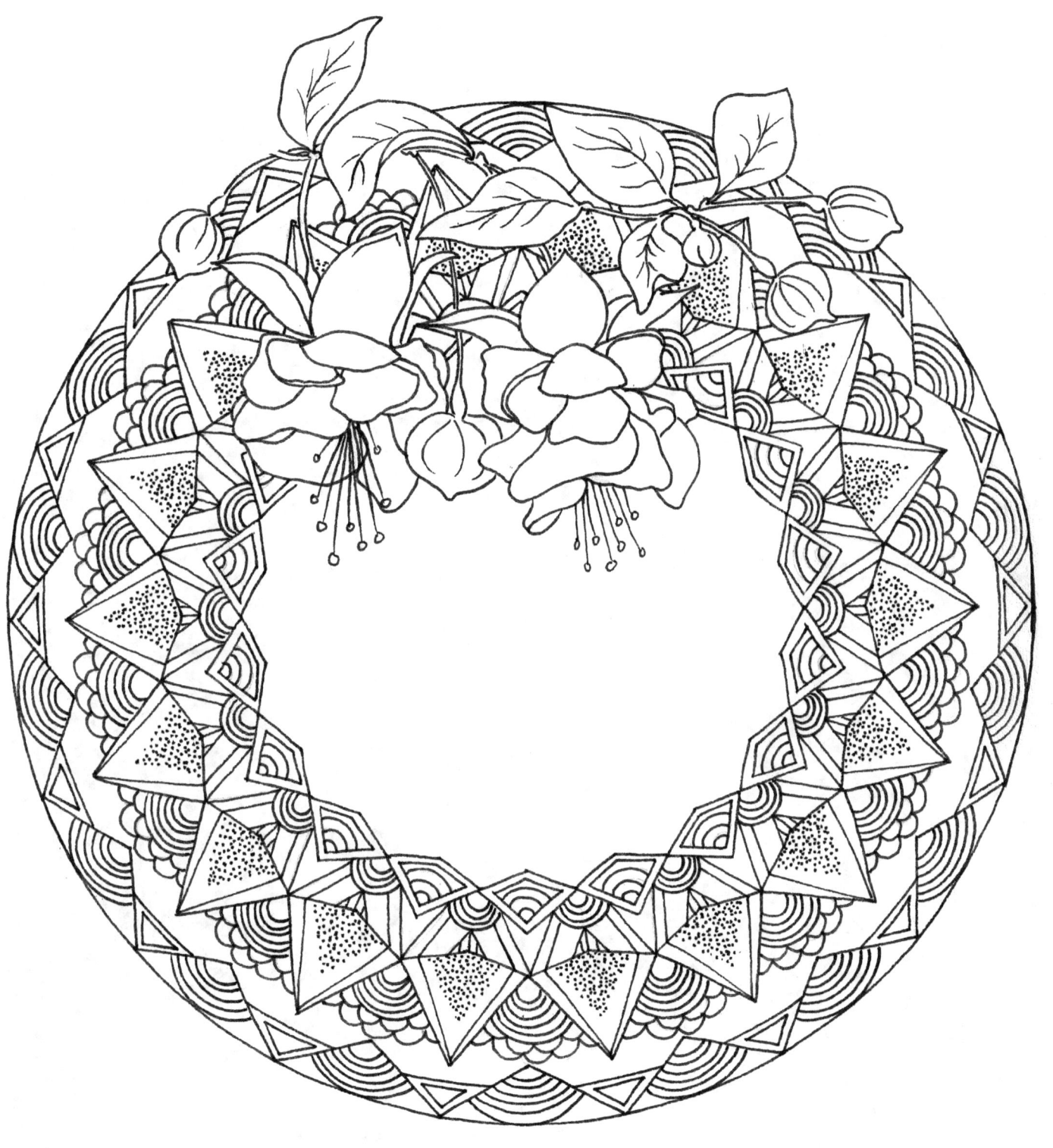

Fuchsia (Onagraceae)

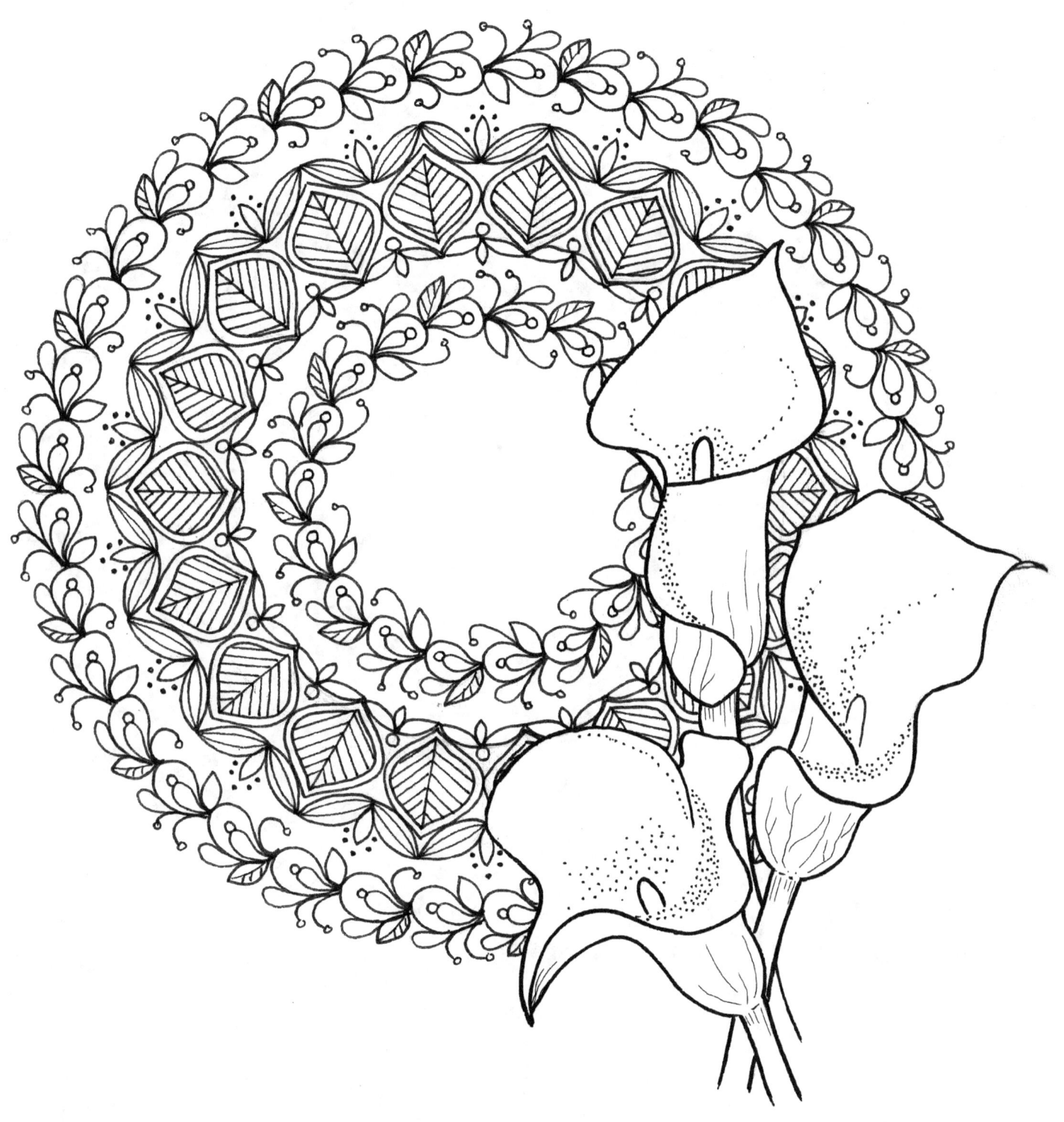

Calla Lily (Zantedeschia Aethiopica)

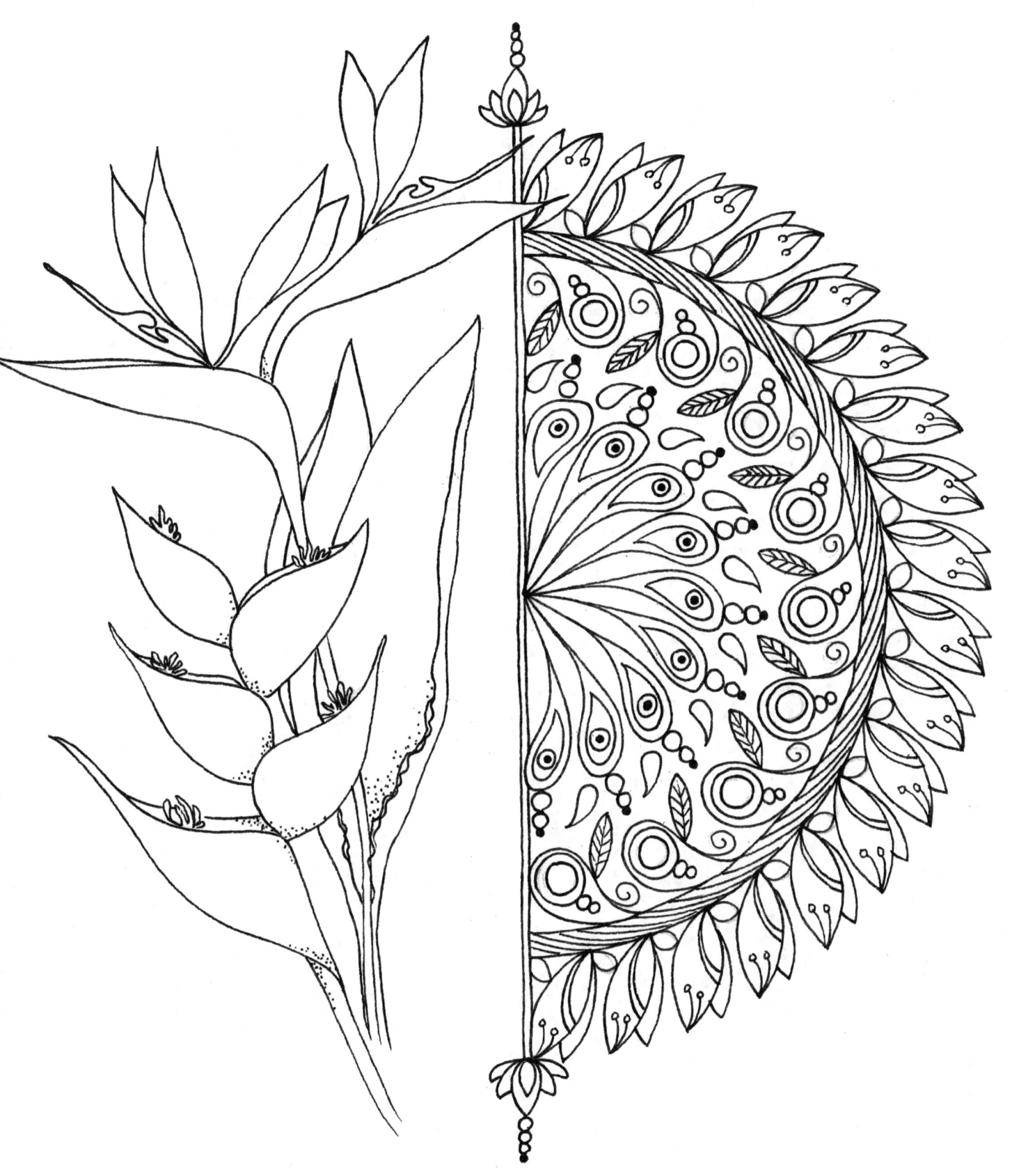

Bird of Paradise (Strelitziaceae)

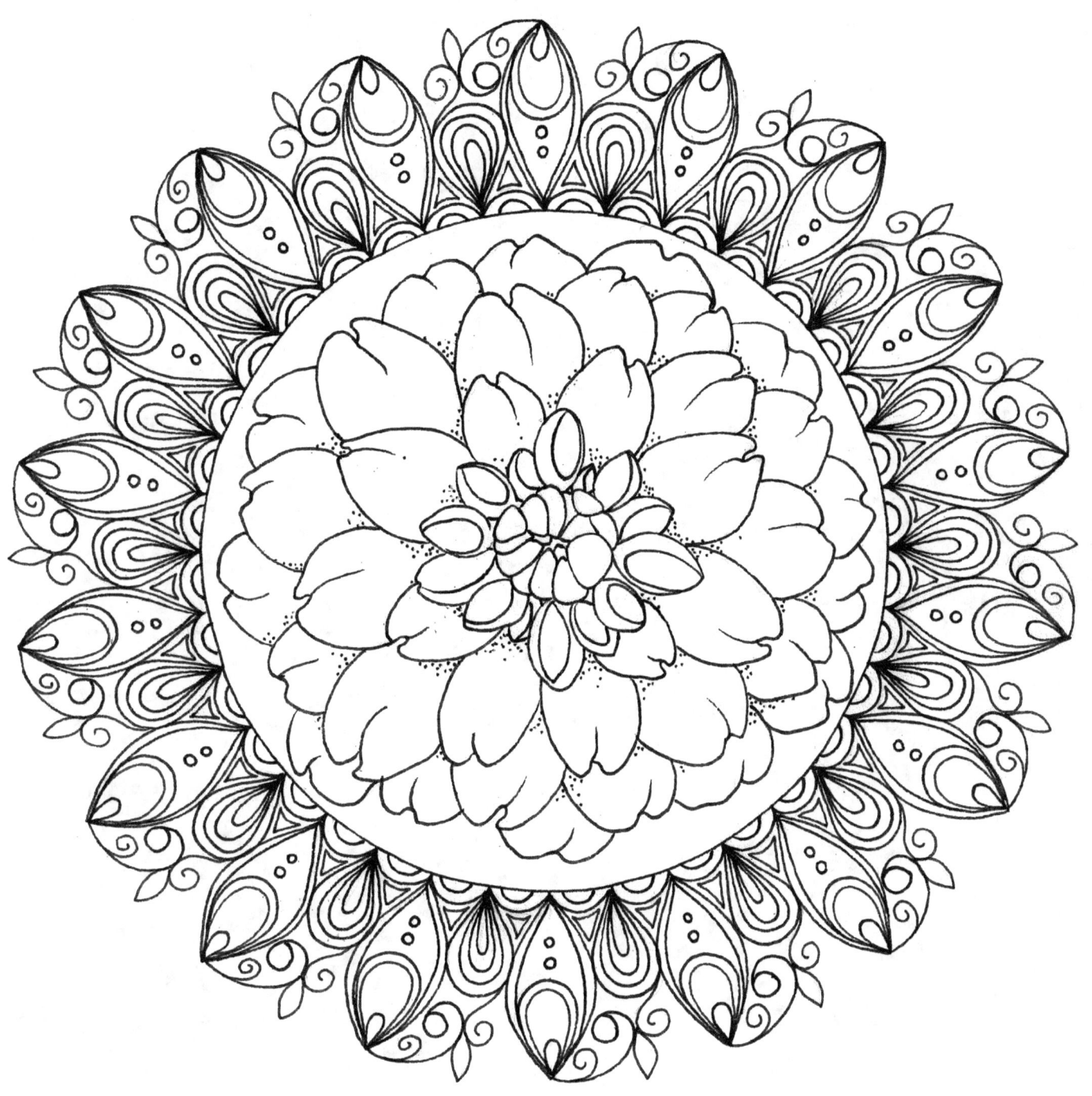

Dahlia (Dahlia Pinnata)

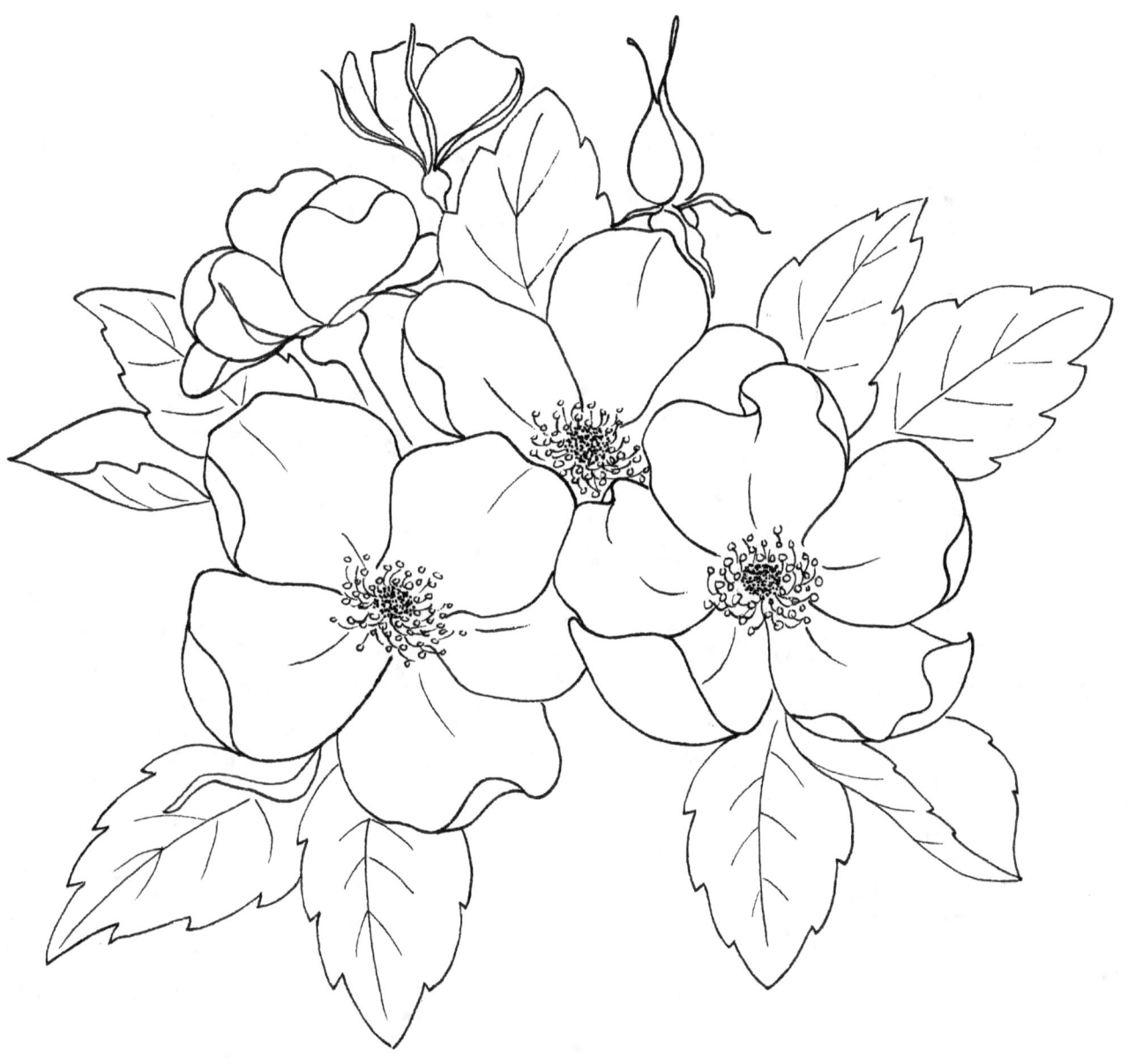

Alberta Wild Rose (Rosa Acicularis)

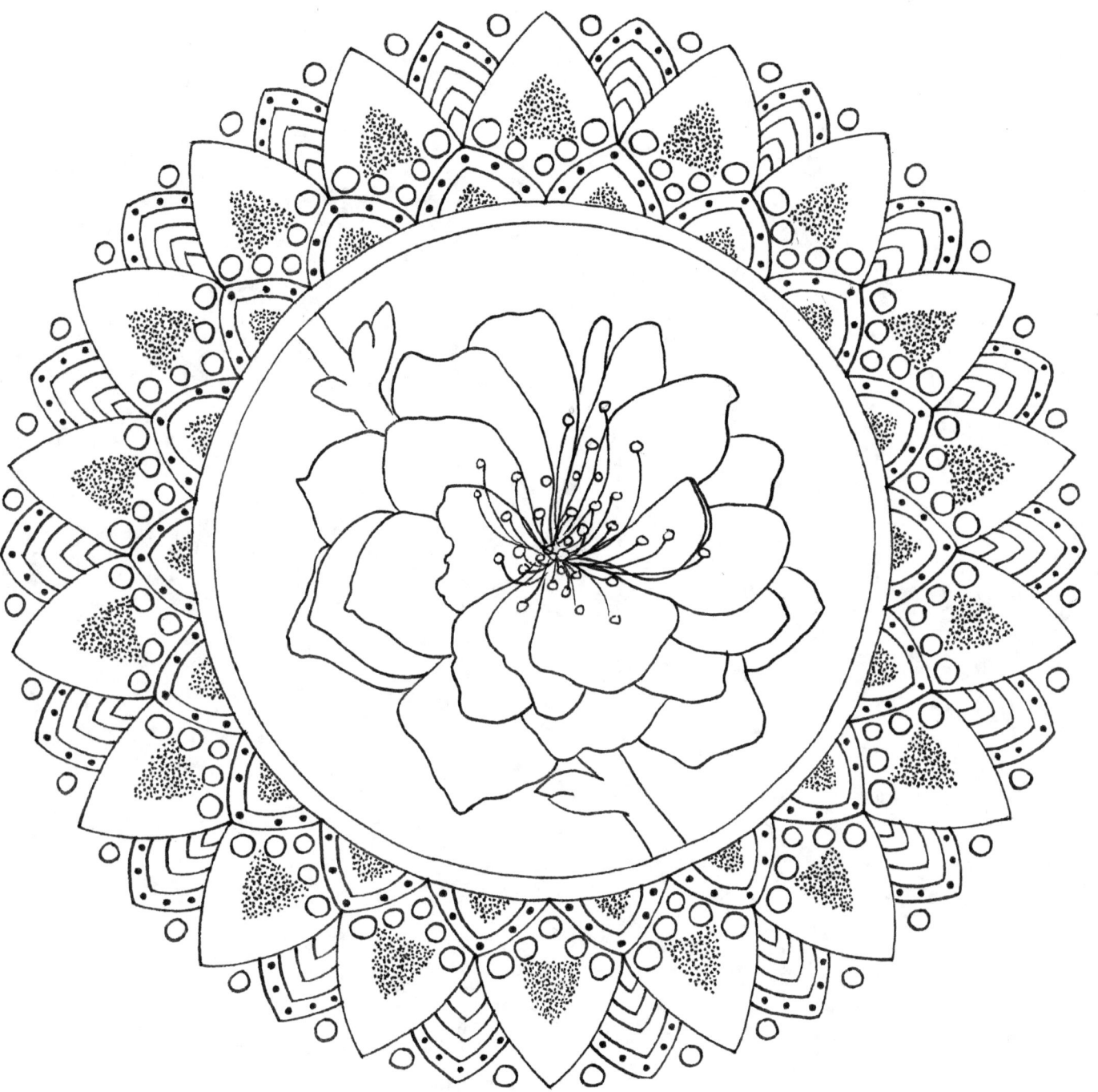

Sakura (Prunus Serrulata)

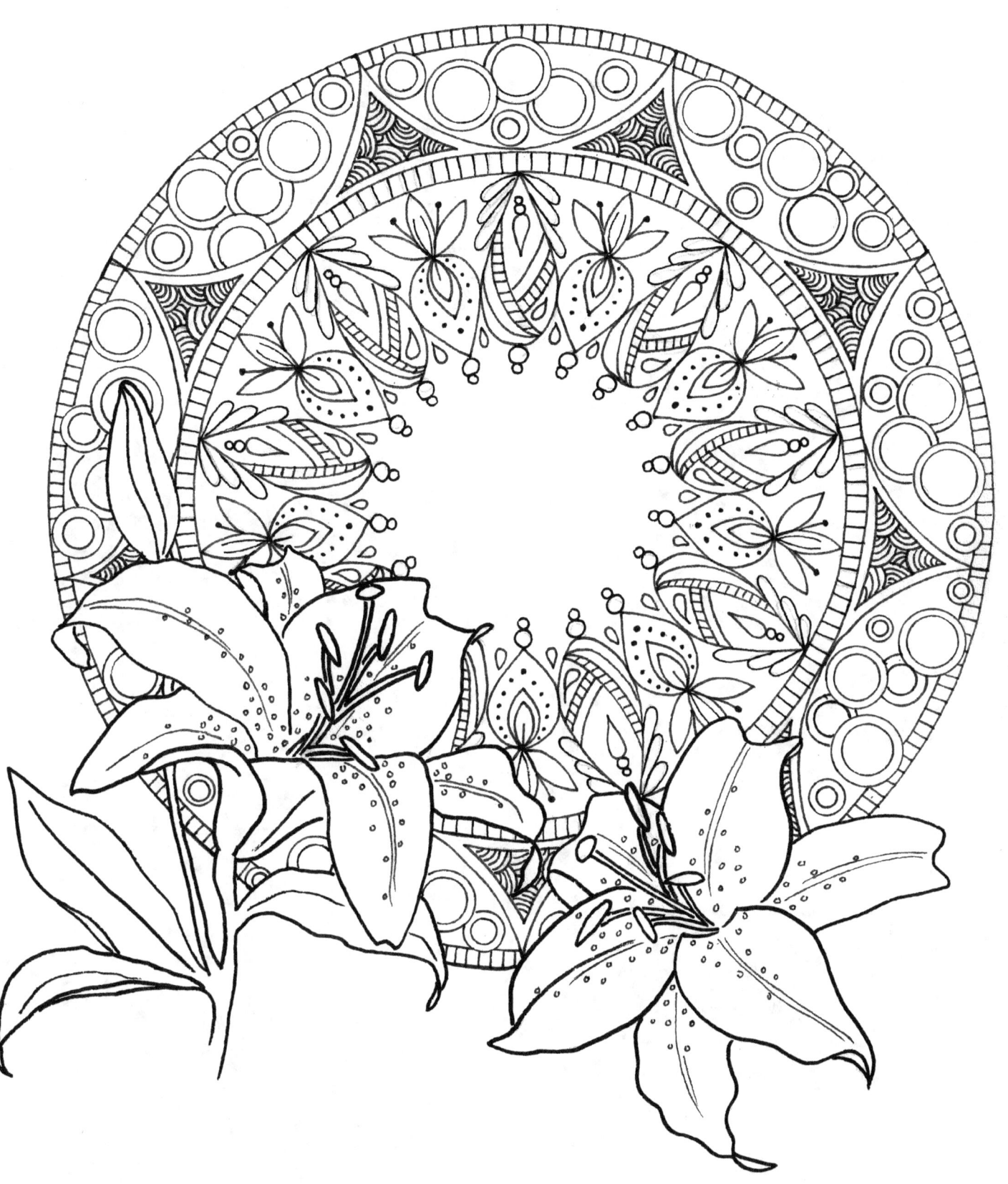

Stargazer Lilies (Lilium Orientalis)

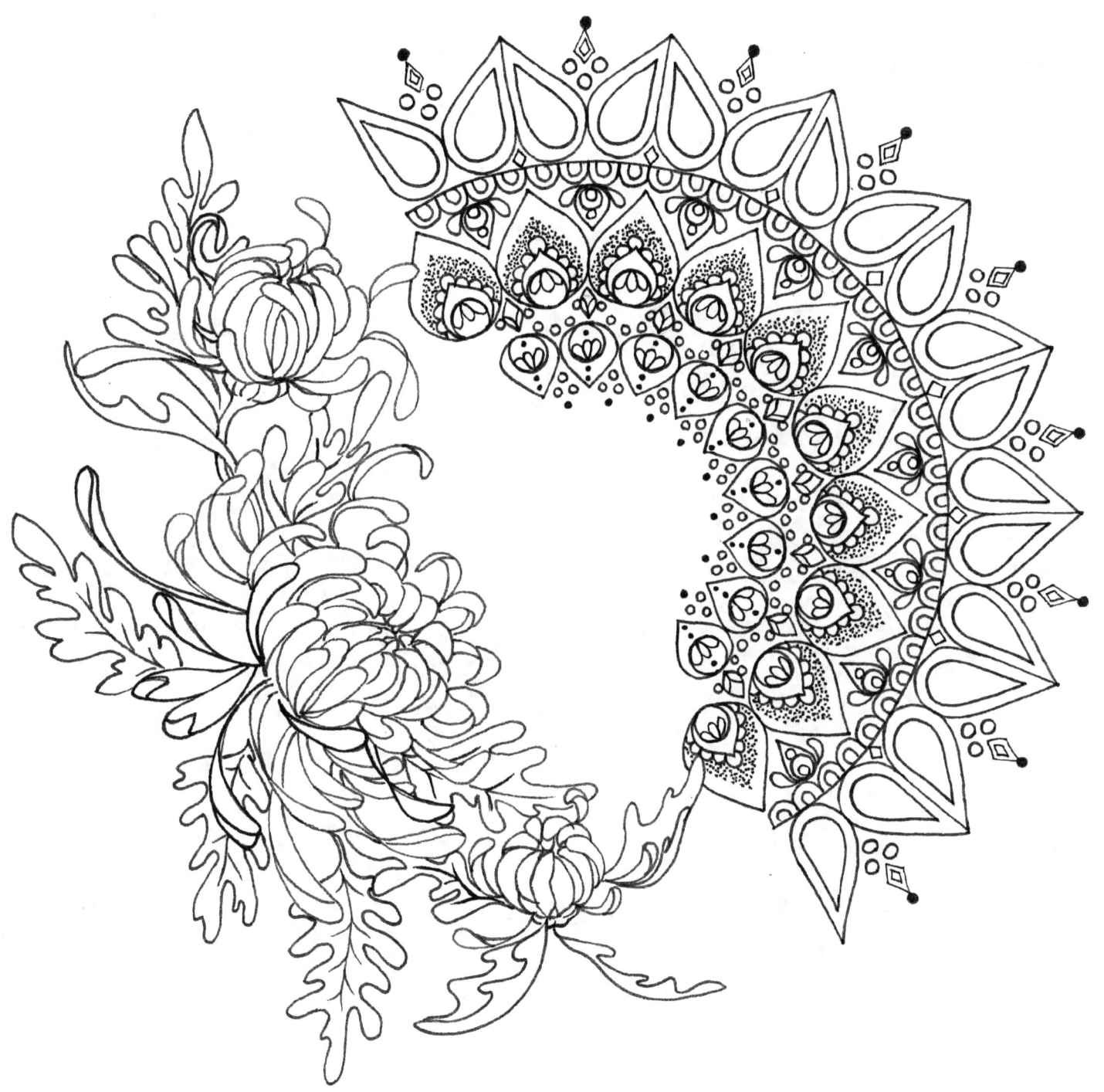

Chrysanthemum (Asteraceae)

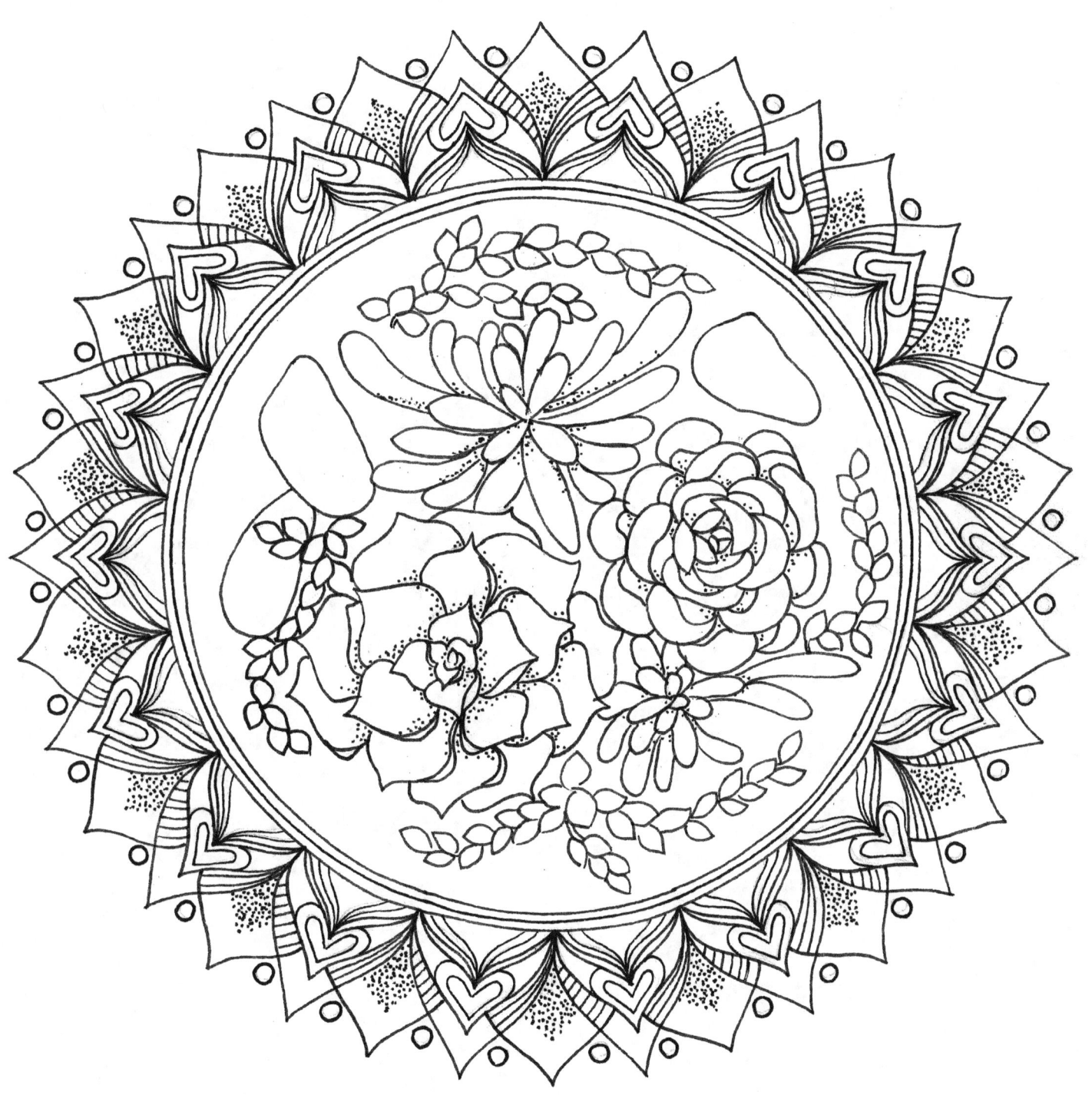

Succulents (Cactaceae)

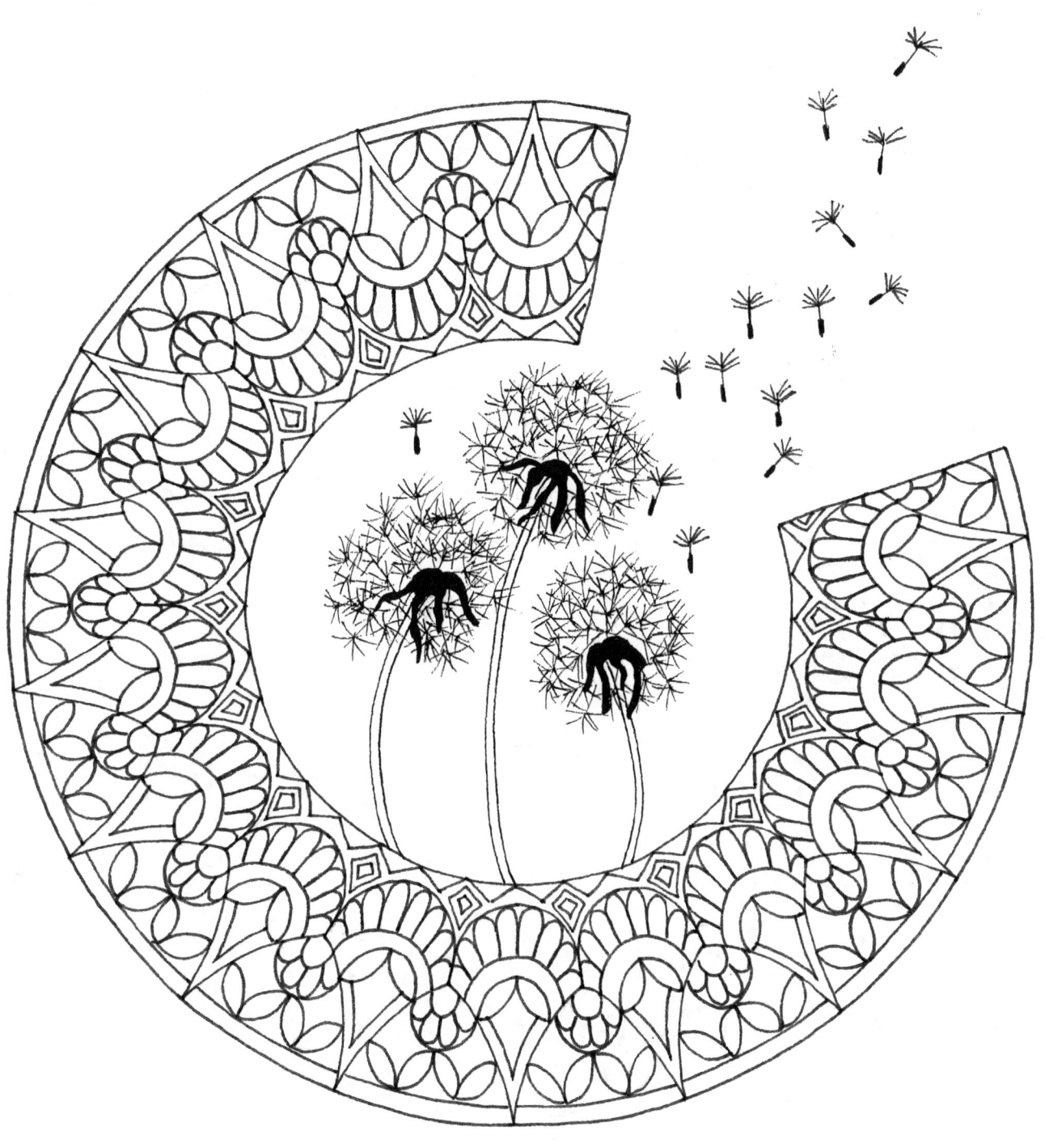

Dandelion (Taraxacum)

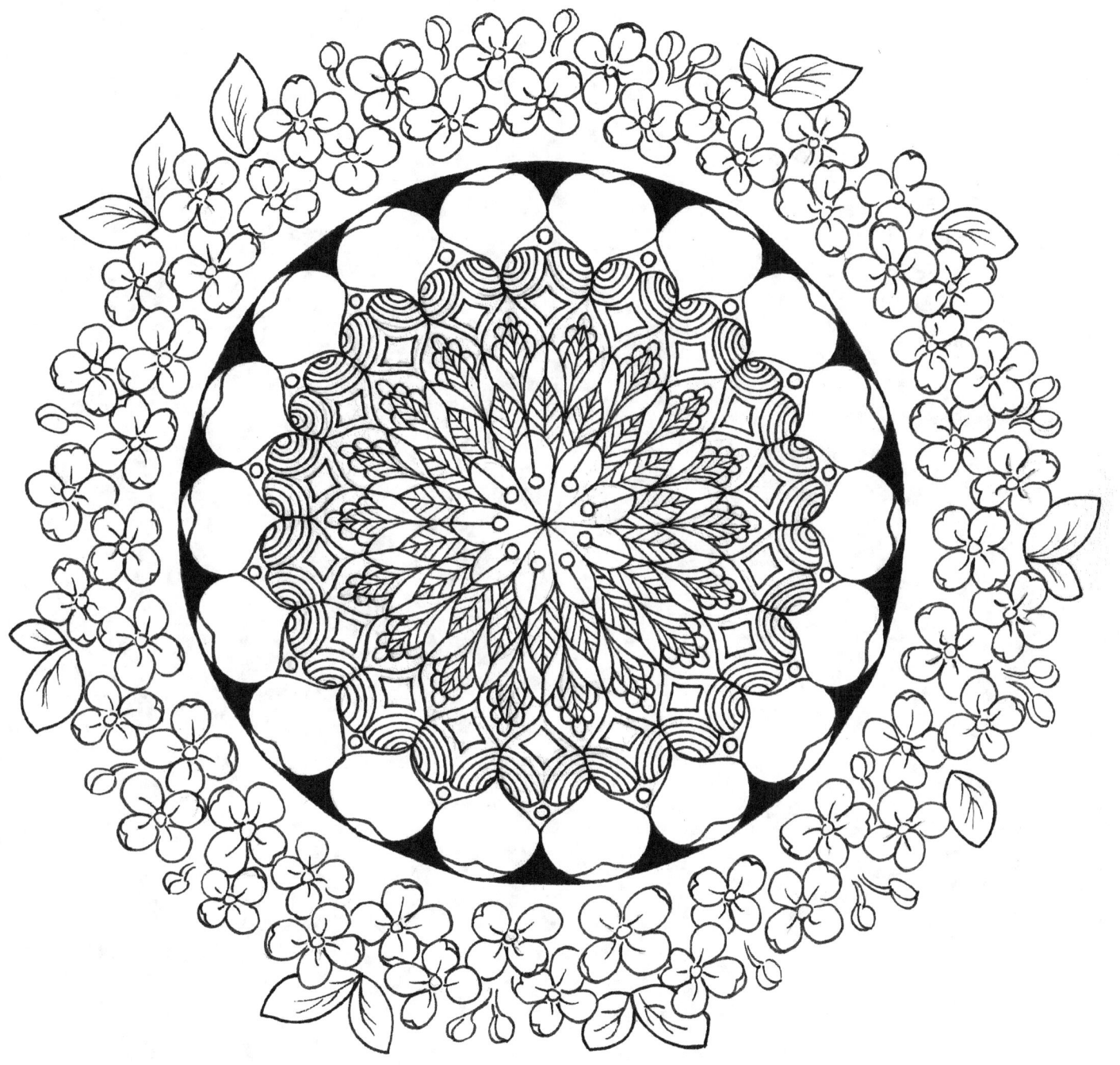

Lilacs (Syringa)

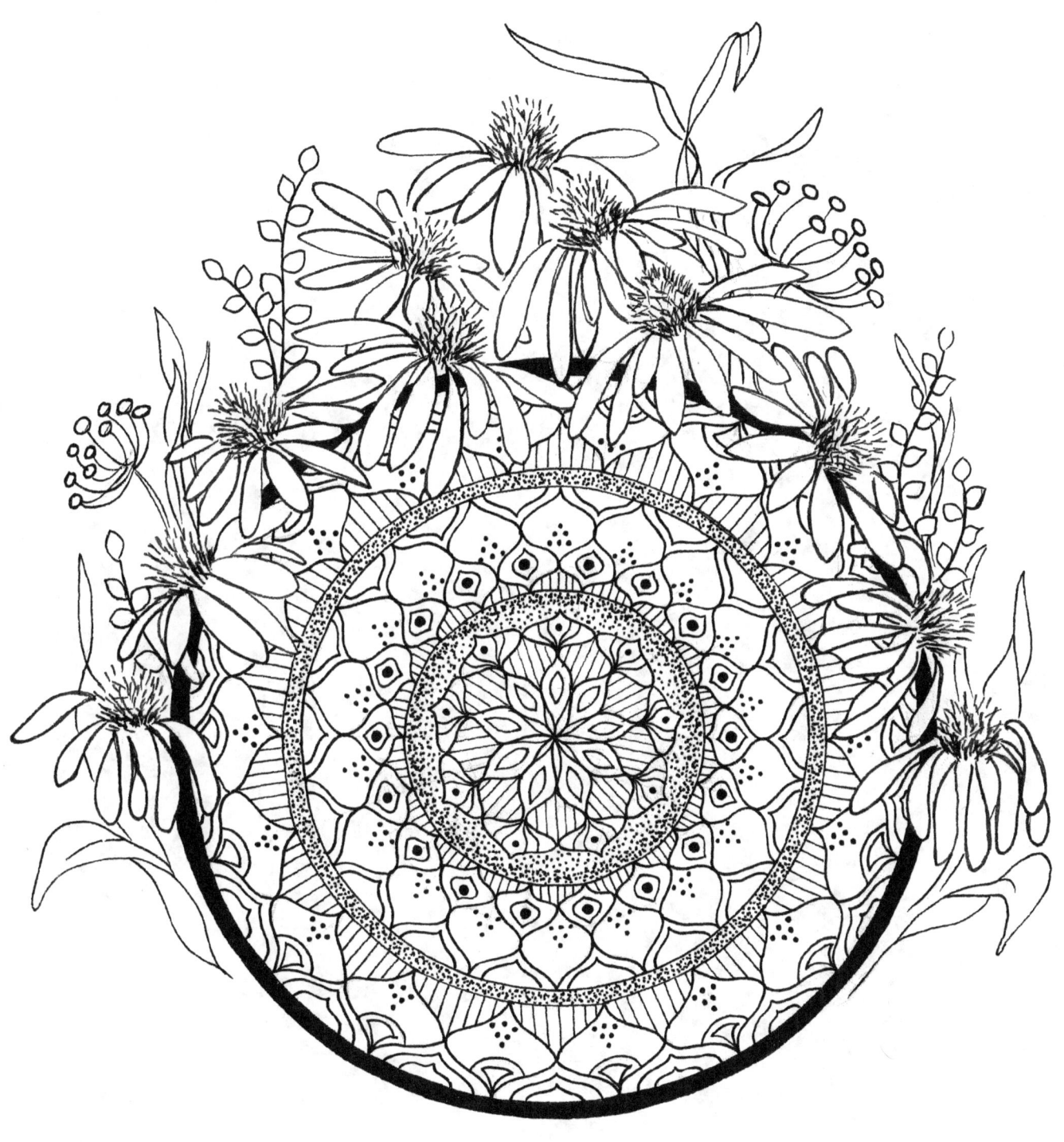

Coneflowers (Echinacea)